THE HAPPY RICKSHAW DRIVER

KIRIT THAKORE

Kirit' Copyright Page
Copyright © 2025 by Kirit Thakore

All rights reserved. No part of this book may be reproduced, stored in a retrieval system, or transmitted in any form or by any means electronic, mechanical, photocopying, recording, or otherwise without prior written permission from the publisher, except for brief quotations in critical reviews or articles.

Published by Kirit Thakore
Leicester, United Kingdom

This is a work of fiction inspired by true events and personal experiences. Names, characters, businesses, places, events, and incidents are either products of the author's imagination or used in a fictitious manner. Any resemblance to actual people, living or dead, or actual events is purely coincidental.

While this book contains advice and techniques for managing stress, it is not intended as a substitute for professional medical advice, diagnosis, or treatment. Always seek the advice of your physician or other qualified health provider with any questions you may have regarding medical condition.

First Edition: 2025
For more information about the author:
Website: kirit.uk
Email: kirit.thakore@gmail.com
Printed in the United Kingdom

Table Of Contents

Introduction _____ 6

Chapter One _____ 8

Chapter Two _____ 16

Chapter Three _____ 25

Chapter Four _____ 31

Chapter Five _____ 36

Chapter Six _____ 40

Chapter Seven _____ 46

Chapter Eight _____ 51

Chapter Nine _____ 60

Chapter Ten _____ 70

Chapter Eleven _____ 79

Final Chapter _____ 94

In conclusion _____ 103

From the author _____ 107

Introduction

Travelling through India is truly a life changing event.

India exposes one to a vibrant, often chaotic, yet deeply humane culture. The concept of **Dharma** (duty or purpose) and **Karma** (the law of cause and effect) are woven into the fabric of daily life and can provide a new lens through which to view one's life choices and challenges. The warmth and hospitality of the Indian people, who often live with a strong sense of community and family, can be a powerful antidote to feelings of isolation and disconnection.

Ultimately, India doesn't just offer a physical journey; it offers a journey inward. For those who feel adrift, the country's ancient wisdom and enduring spirit can be a guiding light, helping them navigate back to their own centre.

I was in Mumbai recently and wanted to see the reaction from my daughter, who had never been there before. She was bewildered by the sounds, the smells, the crowds, the acceptance of it all and so much more. I could see her eyes grow larger and brighter with every happening.

We jumped into a rickshaw and off we went. In an instant, she was mesmerised. In fact, almost hypnotised by India. I watched her and realised that she was there, she was there in that moment. Lost to every problem she had ever had. In that moment I felt her soul, her spirit being lifted. In that moment I knew this could be the solution to life. In that moment "The Happy Rickshaw Driver" was born. Enjoy the journey.

Chapter One

The cabin doors released with a sigh, as though the plane itself was relieved to be finished with its journey, and the first breath of Mumbai rolled in. Heat surged forward, humid and heavy, carrying with it the tang of jet fuel and something metallic, like rust stirred into air. Hansa adjusted the strap of her laptop bag against her blazer, her blouse clinging at the collar already. Her fellow passengers shuffled toward the jet bridge with the kind of weary urgency that always followed long flights.

She followed, her carry-on thumping over the thin carpet. The air shifted step by step, from the cool sterility of the aircraft to the damp, unfiltered weight of the city. Kerosene, mildew, damp concrete, it all pressed into her skin. Her carefully straightened hair surrendered in moments, curls springing free around her temples. She smoothed them back automatically, a gesture of habit, though she knew it was pointless. Tomorrow, under stage lights, she would be speaking to a room of delegates about the damage stress inflicts on the human body. Tonight, she felt like a case study walking on her own two feet.

Immigration was a bottleneck of bodies and impatience. A man ahead of her argued loudly with an officer about a missing signature; the family behind her jostled and whispered, the youngest child tugging at her skirt hem until the mother hissed him back into place. The air was sharp with disinfectant and sweat. Each stamp of the official's hand came down like a gavel: sharp, final, unyielding.

Hansa rolled her shoulders and tried to focus on her breath. In. Out.

Her presentation slides would open with a simple image: the human nervous system under siege. She had written the line herself: *Stress is the body's fire alarm. The danger is when the alarm never stops ringing.* Standing here, under the fluorescent buzz, her chest tight and her palms damp, she thought grimly that Mumbai's airport seemed to embody the metaphor. The alarm wasn't just ringing; it was blaring from every wall.

She cleared immigration, collected her suitcase, and followed the flow toward the sliding glass doors. And then, suddenly, overwhelmingly, she was in it.

The arrivals hall crashed over her like a surf. Noise rose in waves, folding over itself until it was impossible to distinguish a single thread. Families cried out, laughter pealed across the space, announcements blared from above in English, Hindi, Marathi, their edges distorted by the speakers. Drivers pressed forward at the railings, holding up signs in blocky black marker: *Mr. Patel, Mohan, Conference Delegates.* Some names were written so faintly they looked like whispers; others screamed in oversized capitals.

Movement surged around her. Children darted between trolleys, shrieking, their shoes slapping on the polished floor. A garland of marigolds landed on a tired traveler's shoulders nearby, the petals scattering to the ground, filling the air with the sharp sweetness of orange bloom.

And the smells, layered, knotted, inescapable. Incense smoke drifting faintly, as if carried in someone's clothes. The sharp, irresistible oil of frying pakoras and samosas from a stall outside. Sweat, warm and human, clinging to every shifting body in the crowd. Diesel seeping in from the road beyond, edged with the briny ghost of the Arabian Sea.

Hansa stopped, just for a moment, her suitcase handle gripped firmly in both hands. She shut her eyes and inhaled. Her chest rose sharply, her heart ticking against her ribs. She thought of the lines she had rehearsed for weeks, words she would deliver to colleagues tomorrow: *Stress corrodes slowly, invisibly, until the system begins to fail.*

But here, now, standing in this collision of sound and scent, she felt something else: not just corrosion, but intensity. Mumbai didn't present itself as calm. It presented itself as survival. A city whose very atmosphere demanded resilience, whose pressure threatened to crush and, at the same time, to forge.

The sliding doors opened again, releasing another tide of passengers, and the sound swelled louder still. Outside, the night unfolded in restless layers. Headlights flashed across the pavement, weaving together like fireflies in panic. Taxi drivers shouted over one another, palms slamming against dented roofs. A woman balanced a plastic crate on her head, her sari pleats hitched up for movement, while her son tugged impatiently at her hand. A stray dog nosed through the litter at the curb, unbothered by the chaos.

The heat was relentless, as if the air itself had substance, pressing insistently against every breath she took. Yet beneath the stickiness, beneath the roar of horns and voices, she could feel something pulsing. Life, fierce and unyielding.

Tomorrow she would speak of the dangers of unrelenting pressure. Tonight she wondered if she was witnessing another truth: that sometimes, under the crush of noise and urgency, people didn't only wither. Sometimes they burned out.

Hansa squared her shoulders, hitched her bag more firmly into place, and stepped into the city's mouth.

A Note From The Author

Thank you for starting this journey with me. If Hansa's story resonates with you, whether it brings you peace, makes you reflect, or simply makes you smile, I would be deeply grateful if you could share your honest thoughts in a brief review on Amazon. Your authentic feedback, even just a few words, helps other readers discover this book and lets me know these words have found their way to the right heart.

- Kirit

Please scan the QR code below to leave a review on Amazon

Amazon UK

Amazon U.S.

Amazon Canada

Chapter Two

The room was quiet, almost too quiet. A cocoon of hotel sterility: white sheets tucked too tightly, a hum from the air-conditioning unit, curtains that shut out the city's endless noise. Hansa lay on her back in the bed, staring at the ceiling, her body stretched out but tense, her mind refusing to rest.

The chatter started as soon as she closed her eyes.

You should be asleep by now. You'll look tired tomorrow. You always look tired these days. How many more conferences can you bluff through before people see what's underneath?

She turned onto her side, pressing her cheek into the cool pillow, but her thoughts followed her. They never really let her go.

Her life had been nothing but layers of strain. The divorce, years ago. The two children she had raised alone, who now lived their lives at a distance, barely calling, offering only the thinnest thread of connection when she reached out first. Her parents, both gone now. Her father taken swiftly, her mother slowly, dementia unraveling her memory thread by fragile thread. Hansa had been the one to care for her, the daughter who sat by the bed in the small hours spooning soup and whispering reassurances to a woman who no longer remembered her name. And when the funeral came, she had felt emptied out, not just of her mother but of her own strength.

And always, always the money. The calculations in notebooks, the skipped luxuries, the endless small sacrifices. This trip had been paid for, yes, but her fee was barely enough to cover a month of groceries. Yet she had accepted because she needed the chance, the exposure, the fragile hope that doors might open if she kept showing up.

But beneath all that, there had been another reason.

India.

She had heard it described in reverent tones, almost mythic. *India transforms everyone.*

People had told her: it was a place of contradictions, yes, but also of healing. A land where saints sat in caves high in the Himalayas and beggars shared their last chapati with strangers. Where rich and poor lived side by side, palaces casting shadows over slums, and yet life thrived in both. Where spirituality was not hidden away but flowed openly, stitched into the everyday, offerings of flowers on cracked pavements, incense drifting from roadside shrines, prayers painted on the sides of buses, the murmur of mantras woven into the marketplace.

She had heard of the great rivers, sacred and yet polluted, carrying ashes and offerings, washing away sins. Of pilgrims who walked barefoot for miles, carrying nothing but faith. Of festivals where the streets blazed with colour, bodies pressed together in ecstatic devotion, faces lit by oil lamps floating on water.

They had spoken of ashrams where silence stretched for weeks, where seekers came from across the world to unlearn themselves. Of gurus with eyes that pierced through the masks people wore, eyes that saw directly into wounds long hidden. Of meditation halls where thousands sat cross-legged in stillness, the sound of a single bell ringing like eternity itself.

India heals you, they had said. *India strips you down and shows you who you really are.*

And lying there, her body aching, her breath shallow, Hansa had wanted to believe it.

Her eyelids grew heavy, her thoughts loosening into half-dreams. She saw flashes of what people had described, though she had never witnessed them herself. A river at dawn, mist rising, the air trembling with the murmur of mantras. Men in saffron robes stepping into the water, their hands pressed together, their eyes lifted to the rising sun. Women in saris bending to release tiny clay lamps onto the current, each flame a fragile heartbeat floating away.

She saw narrow lanes crowded with people and cows, shopkeepers setting out brass bowls filled with marigolds, the smell of incense rising from shrines tucked into crumbling walls. She felt the press of a crowd at a festival, paint and powder bursting in colours she could not name, her laughter rising with theirs, her body no longer heavy but light, alive.

In this half-dream India, she was not bent beneath her burdens. She was porous, open, dissolving into the rush of sound and colour, as though the city itself had drawn the pain out of her and replaced it with something fierce and luminous.

Her breath deepened. The images shimmered, then slipped away, replaced again by the ceiling of her hotel room and the steady hum of the air-conditioning.

She turned, restless, sighing into the darkness. Maybe transformation didn't come in a single night. Maybe it wasn't in the city, or the temples, or the crowds, but in the slow, reluctant loosening of her own grip.

Mumbai didn't pretend to be serene. It wore its chaos openly, without apology. Perhaps that was its lesson: healing might not mean silence, but the courage to stand in the storm without breaking.

Her eyes grew heavy, and soon she slipped into that fragile space between waking and dreaming.

She found herself standing at the edge of a wide river. Dawn stretched pale across the sky, the air cool, the surface of the water trembling with the faintest ripples. Bells rang in the distance, slow, resonant, steady. Pilgrims moved past her, stepping into the river with cupped hands and bowed heads, their voices murmuring prayers in rhythms she didn't understand but somehow felt in her chest.

A holy man approached, wrapped in saffron cloth, ash smeared across his forehead. His eyes were dark, unblinking, and when they fell on her, she felt pinned, as though he could see the fatigue etched in her bones, the grief pressed into her skin. He did not speak at first. He only looked, and the silence between them was weightier than any word.

Finally, his lips parted. His voice was soft, yet it carried like the river itself.

"You are carrying too much."

Hansa tried to reply, but her throat was thick. Her eyes stung.

"You clutch it as though it is who you are," the man continued. "But pain is not identity. Grief is not identity. They are seasons. You have mistaken the storm for the sky."

She wanted to argue, to say that she couldn't simply put down what had been hers to bear for decades, her children, her parents, the debts, the endless duties. But her voice wouldn't form. Instead, she felt something within her unclench, just slightly, as though the river itself was tugging at the weight she carried.

And then she saw her mother. Not as she had been at the end, lost and frail, but as she once was: laughing, her hair pinned back, her eyes sharp and alive. She stood on the riverbank across from Hansa, her hand raised in greeting, her mouth forming words Hansa could not hear. Yet somehow she understood: *Let go, sweetheart. Live your life now.*

The image shimmered, dissolved into water and light. The holy man, too, faded, until there was only the river, stretching wide, carrying lamps downstream, tiny flames that trembled but did not extinguish.

Hansa woke with a gasp, her heart pounding, her skin damp. The hotel room came back into focus: the sound of the air-conditioning, the heavy stillness of the curtains. She lay back slowly, one hand pressed to her chest.

Dream or imagination, it didn't matter. The words clung to her. *You have mistaken the storm for the sky.*

She stared at the ceiling, her breath unsteady, and wondered if India had already begun its work on her.

Tomorrow she would put on her blazer, smooth her hair, stand on a stage, and speak about stress as though she were the master of the subject. They would nod and write down her words. And yet deep inside, she knew that something had already shifted, that the land people spoke of as transformative had, in the space of one strange night, reached into her restless mind and whispered a truth she could no longer ignore.

Chapter Three

For the first time in what felt like years, Hansa had slept. Deep, uninterrupted sleep, the kind that left her muscles unknotted and her mind quiet. She awoke slowly, blinking at the soft morning light creeping through the hotel curtains, and felt... lighter. Not entirely unburdened, but for the first time in a long while, she sensed that something, maybe the air, maybe the city itself, was seeping into her, filling spaces she hadn't realised were empty.

She stretched, arms above her head, listening to the low hum of Mumbai outside her window. The city was already awake, alive in ways that startled her, honking horns, a shout from a street vendor, the rhythmic sound of tyres against pavement. And yet, beneath it all, there was something different this morning. She felt steadier, as though the chaos beyond her walls had been softened, absorbed by some unseen current, leaving her lighter, more present.

Breakfast could wait. Today, she had to get to the conference venue. Normally, she would have taken a taxi, predictable, easy, but her friends had insisted she try something more local.

"Take a rickshaw," one had said. "It's the best way to see the city. You'll feel it."

Stepping outside, Hansa was greeted by a sensory symphony. The street buzzed with life: dozens of rickshaws weaving between buses and cars, bicycles balancing precariously on the edges of traffic, pedestrians sidestepping the chaos with a practiced ease. Vendors shouted their wares, bananas, chai, plastic-wrapped sweets and somewhere, a bell rang from a nearby temple. The smell of frying snacks mingled with diesel fumes, with the faint sweetness of marigolds from the flower stalls.

And then there were the colours.

The greens and yellows of the rickshaws shone in the sunlight, flaking paint revealing the stories of decades. Women walked past, saris trailing like rivers of jewel tones, emeralds, sapphires, rubies, and citrine that swirled around them as they moved. Fruit stands glimmered with oranges, pomegranates, and the bright reds of chilli peppers stacked in pyramids. Temple flags snapped in the breeze, orange and maroon and saffron, fluttering above doorways painted in every shade of turquoise, pink, and mustard. Even the pavement seemed alive, washed with dust and chalk and spilled spices, flecked with colour at every step.

Hansa felt her chest lift slightly. The sheer richness of it, the audacity of colour layered on chaos, struck something in her she hadn't felt in years. It wasn't just beauty, it was life, raw and unfiltered, daring her to breathe it in.

Among the dozens of rickshaws, one pulled slightly to the side, its paint fresh and gleaming. The driver sat straight, eyes bright and steady. When she looked at him, he smiled, not a forced, practiced smile, but a calm, open one that seemed to make the world pause.

"Hello madam," he said, his voice warm, rolling across the cacophony like a soft bell. "My name is Kirit. Where can I take you?"

Hansa felt a strange serenity wash over her. The noise, the honking, the swirl of people, everything seemed to recede around him, as if his presence created a pocket of calm. She smiled back, a small, genuine curve of lips that she hadn't worn in a long time.

"Take me to the Mumbai Exhibition Centre," she said, her voice lighter than she expected.

Kirit nodded, checking the rickshaw for balance, then leaned forward to start. The engine hummed, the vehicle shifting smoothly into the flow of traffic. And as the city moved around them, Hansa felt herself moving differently too. Slower, more aware, absorbing the life around her without the usual tension clutching at her chest.

The city unfolded like a living painting. She noticed the vibrant sari of a woman negotiating fruit from a stall, the fuchsia powder smeared across a temple wall, the glint of sunlight on brass vessels in a roadside shrine. Rickshaws darted past, their bright banners flapping in the wind. Even the beggars, the children running barefoot across the streets, seemed part of the tapestry, moving in rhythm with the city's pulse.

And with every turn, every honk and shout, every flicker of colour, Hansa felt herself absorbing it. Lightness. Presence. Something she had not felt in years. Something she almost dared to call hope.

Kirit navigated the streets effortlessly, weaving through the chaos with a calm certainty. Every time he glanced at her, there was a softness in his eyes, an understanding without words. Hansa realised she could breathe more freely with him beside her, that the tension in her shoulders was easing, that the ache in her chest had loosened just enough to let the city flow through her.

For the first time in decades, she felt like a participant in the world rather than a woman being crushed under it.

The colours, the sounds, the scents, they weren't assaulting her senses; they were teaching her, showing her that life could be vivid and overwhelming and still nourishing. And somewhere in the weaving chaos, in the bright yellows and rich oranges, in the fluttering temple flags, Hansa felt a whisper of something she had almost forgotten: a sense that she could, finally, find her way back to herself.

Chapter Four

The rickshaw swayed gently beneath her as Kirit weaved into the river of Mumbai traffic, and Hansa felt herself suspended in a current of life unlike anything she had ever experienced. The city roared around her, a riot of movement, noise, and colour that pressed in from every direction.

Lorries thundered past, their wheels thumping against the asphalt, horns blaring, engines coughing up clouds of smoke that stung her eyes. Motorbikes darted in between, carrying entire families on a single bike: fathers gripping handlebars, mothers balanced sideways behind them, children clinging with fierce concentration. Every pass seemed impossibly close, yet somehow, no one collided.

Luxury cars gleamed beside beat-up Ambassador taxis, their paint chipped and engines wheezing, all competing for the same impossible space. Rickshaws darted in and out like insects, horns blaring in a chaotic rhythm, while pedestrians wove through gaps with astonishing confidence, some stepping off the curb into the maelstrom without hesitation.

Cows ambled lazily between vehicles, tails swishing, impervious to the chaos. Goats trotted along the edge of the street, sniffing at discarded bags, and dogs threaded nimbly between wheels, disappearing as quickly as they appeared.

Slum children lined the sidewalks, playing with tires, tin cans, or scraps of cardboard, sometimes spilling onto the road, laughing and shouting, weaving around trucks and scooters with the familiarity of long practice. Street vendors leaned from the backs of trucks or balanced precariously on carts, calling out their wares: steaming chai, fresh fruit, bundles of marigolds, packets of fried snacks. Beggars approached vehicles, pressing palms against windows, murmuring prayers or pleas, their children clinging to their sides.

Horns blared endlessly. Horns demanded. Horns warned. Horns sang. Hansa realised she could no longer separate the sound from the motion; it was a language of the city, urgent and constant.

Colours assaulted her in waves. The rickshaw zipped past women in saris of fuchsia, turquoise, and gold, fabric trailing in arcs that seemed to linger in the air long after they passed. Fruit stalls blazed with the reds and yellows of mangos, pomegranates, and chilies. Temple flags waved above doorways, fluttering over pastel-painted buildings. Even the pavement seemed alive, streaked with dust, chalk, and spilled spices.

And yet, somehow, inside Kirit's rickshaw, there was calm. He guided them through the storm with a quiet certainty, hands steady on the handlebars, eyes alert but serene. Hansa felt herself drawn into that calm, the tension in her shoulders softening, her chest rising and falling with ease. The chaos surrounded her but didn't touch her.

She marvelled at it all, the fearless audacity of the people, the resilience of the city, the way life pushed forward in every shape and colour, against every expectation of order. It was overwhelming, exhilarating, and terrifying, yet beneath it all was a rhythm she could feel in her bones.

She thought of her children, of the years of sacrifice and the loneliness that had followed. She thought of her mother, of nights spent at a bedside, and of herself, worn down by stress and loss. And yet, for the first time in years, she felt a flicker of something new: the possibility that life could still be vibrant, that she could still move with it rather than be crushed by it.

The city wasn't assaulting her senses, it was inviting her to notice, to breathe, to be present.

Mumbai's streets, with their horns, vendors, animals, and dazzling colours, became a mirror. If this city could survive, thrive, and even sing amidst such chaos, perhaps she could, too. She could carry her grief and still find joy. She could face stress and still breathe. She could navigate the unpredictable, messy streets of life, and maybe even feel alive along the way.

Kirit steered the rickshaw past another patchwork of vendors, children, and honking vehicles, and Hansa leaned back, closing her eyes briefly. A laugh slipped out of her, soft, unbidden, yet full and true. The city moved around her, relentless and alive, and for the first time, she felt not like an outsider, not like someone being carried under the weight of life, but like a watcher, a witness, a woman finally breathing in rhythm with the world.

Mumbai, in all its chaos, colour, and contradictions, had begun to work its subtle magic.

Chapter Five

Hansa blinked and realised she had been staring. She had been watching Kirit as he manoeuvred the rickshaw with effortless ease, his eyes calm, his posture relaxed, his hands steady on the handlebars as though he were gliding through a dream rather than the relentless chaos of Mumbai's streets.

"Everything okay, madam?" Kirit asked, his voice calm, warm, carrying no hint of impatience. His glance flicked toward her, eyes sharp yet kind, and Hansa felt a sudden jolt, startled out of her reverie.

"Ah... yes," she stammered, cheeks warming. "how on earth do you manage to drive in all this?" She gestured vaguely at the streets: the honking cars, weaving motorbikes, shouting vendors, cows and goats wandering freely, children darting in and out of traffic, the endless stream of pedestrians moving as if gravity didn't exist.

Kirit smiled faintly, almost as if he expected the question. "It is… something you learn," he said slowly, his eyes still scanning the street, aware of everything at once. "You watch. You feel. You trust that others will watch, feel, trust too.

Kirit's eyes met hers briefly, calm and steady. "It is energy," he said simply. "You do not fight it. You do not resist. You move with it, and it carries you. Some days are harder, yes. But you learn to ride the rhythm, to trust it. Then it does not overwhelm you."

Hansa's chest loosened as she listened. There was something in his presence that made the chaos feel less threatening, less overwhelming. She realised she wasn't gripping the edge of the seat, wasn't tensing at every horn, every sudden swerve. It was almost as if Kirit carried a calm bubble with him. A shield against the madness, and somehow, simply by sitting in it, she felt it too.

"How... do you not fear having an accident?" she asked, voice softer now, almost shy. "With all this... everything?"

Kirit shrugged lightly, a gesture so small it seemed casual, yet it spoke volumes. "Fear doesn't help. You cannot control the streets by fear. You watch, you anticipate, you move. You respect the chaos, yes, but you do not fight it. And somehow... everyone else does the same. Somehow it works. Somehow it moves forward."

Hansa's mind spun, struggling to comprehend. How could anyone be so stress-free in the midst of this? The smell of diesel and spices, the roar of engines, the constant clash of metal, the honking and shouting. It would have frayed her nerves within minutes if she had been at the wheel. Yet here he was, steady, confident, present. And she realised that, somehow, in his presence, the city seemed less hostile, less chaotic.

She found herself studying him again, feeling a strange mix of awe and relief. There was a rhythm to the way he moved, a quiet grace in the way he navigated the madness. Watching him, she could almost forget the fear, the tension, the constant calculating of danger that usually occupied her mind in moments like this.

"Teach me," she said, almost whispering, more to herself than to him. "I want to feel like that. I want to… move through it, not be crushed by it."

Kirit's eyes met hers in the rearview mirror. His calm smile didn't change. "Perhaps," he said softly, "you already are."

And in that moment, Hansa realised that for the first time in years, she didn't feel only like a passenger in the world. She felt like she could learn to ride with it, too.

Chapter Six

The rickshaw slowed and then pulled neatly to the side of the road. Hansa looked around, puzzled. They had stopped beside a small stall, no bigger than a wardrobe, painted in peeling blue, with pots of oil bubbling and trays of golden pastries stacked high. The air was thick with the aroma of frying spices, roasted chilies, and freshly brewed tea.

"What are you doing?" Hansa asked, leaning forward, half-amused, half-confused.

Kirit turned to her with that same unshakable calm, his smile as warm as the morning sun. "Madam, you cannot give a talk on an empty stomach," he said simply. "I heard your tummy rumbling."

Hansa blinked, then laughed in disbelief. "How could you possibly hear that? With all this noise?" She gestured around them: the horns, the vendors shouting, the clatter of pans, the cries of children.

"But I have to get to the conference centre," explained Hansa.

"Don't worry madam, we won't be long."

Kirit just smiled wider, saying nothing more, and stepped down from the rickshaw.

Before she could protest, he was at the counter, speaking rapid Hindi to the vendor, who reached into a vat of hot oil and pulled out two steaming samosas, crisp and golden. Beside them, a boy poured tea from a dented kettle into small glass cups, the chai swirling with milk and sugar, steam rising into the air fragrant with cardamom and ginger.

Kirit motioned for her to follow, and she reluctantly slid out of the rickshaw. He guided her to a makeshift table, an uneven wooden plank propped on old crates, and set two tiny plastic stools beside it. Hansa hesitated before sitting, her business suit out of place against the dusty roadside, but Kirit's presence steadied her. She sat, and the stool wobbled slightly beneath her.

The vendor set down the samosas, the pastry crisp and glistening, alongside the hot, sweet chai. Hansa picked one up, its heat searing her fingers, and broke it open. Steam escaped, carrying the scent of spiced potatoes and peas, coriander and chilli. She took a bite, and the flavours exploded on her tongue, hot, sharp, tangy, comforting. She let out a small gasp of delight, and Kirit chuckled softly, sipping his tea.

It was then she noticed the scene unfolding beside them. A sleek black Mercedes pulled up to the stall, gleaming even under the layer of city dust. A man stepped out, his shoes polished, his shirt pressed, his watch glinting in the sun. Without hesitation, he ordered his tea and samosas and lowered himself onto a stool identical to Hansa's.

Moments later, another man approached, his shirt torn, his trousers patched, his feet bare and coated in dust. He, too, ordered, counting coins carefully before receiving his food. He sat directly beside the man from the

Mercedes, their elbows nearly touching. Neither looked at the other. Both sipped chai, both ate samosas, both turned their faces toward the street, watching the same traffic pass.

Hansa stared, astonished. Only in India, she thought, could such worlds collide without resistance. A man from the slums and a wealthy businessman, sharing the same table, eating the same food, drinking from the same glasses washed in the same battered bucket. No one blinked. No one questioned it.

Here, the barriers that governed life in other places, wealth, class, status, seemed to dissolve in the swirl of chai steam and frying spices. Hunger was hunger, tea was tea, and for these few moments, everyone was equal.

She felt a tightness rise in her chest, but not from stress this time. From longing. How many years had she eaten alone? How many mornings had she rushed through a meal, distracted by bills, obligations, silence? Her children no longer called unless she did. Her parents were gone. She had become used to sitting at tables that felt too big, plates that went half-finished, conversations that echoed only in her mind.

And yet, here, at this rickety table on the side of a dusty road, she felt surrounded by something she had forgotten existed, connection. Not personal, not directed at her, but present all around. Strangers shared food, space, laughter, without question. For a brief moment, she was part of something wider than herself, something warm and ordinary, yet profoundly healing.

Kirit sipped his tea, watching her with quiet amusement. He didn't explain. He didn't need to. The scene itself was the lesson, and Hansa was already absorbing it.

She realised that India had a way of stripping life down to its essentials. Hunger and food. Thirst and tea. A moment shared, no matter who you were or what you owned. And she wondered if this, more than temples or mantras, was the true spirituality of the country. The selflessness, the acceptance, the simple humanity that bound people together across all divides.

Hansa cradled her warm glass of chai in both hands and smiled, not at Kirit, not at the vendor, not at the men beside her, but simply at being alive in this moment. For the first time in years, she didn't feel so alone.

Chapter Seven

They lingered at the roadside stall long after the samosas had been eaten, the empty plates stacked to one side, the last swirls of sweet chai clinging to their glasses. Around them, the noise of the street continued unabated, horns blaring, vendors calling, children shouting, motorbikes weaving, but at the little table balanced on crates, there was an odd stillness, as if the world had carved out a quiet space just for them.

Kirit leaned back slightly, watching her with that steady, unreadable expression. "Tell me, madam," he asked, his voice gentle but direct, "when you were in the rickshaw, how did you feel? With all the turbulence around you, the traffic, the horns, the madness, what was happening inside you?"

Hansa blinked, caught off guard. She toyed with the rim of her glass, tracing a finger over the faint crack in the side. Her instinct was to shrug it off, but something in his gaze held her.

"I felt..." She hesitated, searching for words. "Calm. Strangely calm. Like I was watching everything without being part of it. The horns, the chaos, the people, the animals. Tt was all there, but it wasn't... pressing on me. I wasn't carrying it."

Kirit's lips curved into a knowing smile. "Yes. You were not holding it. You were only seeing. That is different."

She nodded slowly, surprised at herself. "Back home, the smallest noise can overwhelm me. A bill arriving, the phone ringing, someone asking for something, it feels heavy, like it's all piling up. But here, with so much happening all at once, I felt... lighter. As if my mind stopped pulling me backwards and forwards. I wasn't in yesterday, I wasn't in tomorrow. I was just here. In the moment."

Her voice caught slightly. "It's been so long since I've felt that. Just being in the now. Just existing."

Kirit sipped the last of his chai before setting the glass down with quiet care. His eyes remained fixed on hers, calm and bright. "That is the gift," he said. "The noise here does not stop. The chaos does not lessen. But in its fullness, something inside you becomes still. The present moment reveals itself. And you see, you are enough. This moment is enough."

Hansa felt her throat tighten, not from stress but from recognition. She thought of the years of rushing, of worrying, of carrying burdens that had aged her body and dulled her spirit. She thought of how she had always fought against the noise of life, trying to silence it, control it, escape it. Yet here, in the middle of India's unrelenting clamour, she had discovered something she had never found in the quiet of her own home: peace.

She looked at the people around her, businessmen, slum dwellers, mothers with children, barefoot boys darting between stalls. All of them moving, surviving, living, in the same space, at the same tables. The world did not pause for them, yet they seemed untroubled. Present. Alive.

Her heart softened as she realised the truth: maybe peace didn't come from silence or from fixing everything. Maybe peace came from being fully here, breathing, watching, letting life happen without resisting it.

Kirit seemed to read her thoughts. He leaned forward slightly, his voice low but firm. "Madam, tomorrow you speak at the Bombay Exhibition Centre, yes? About stress?"

She nodded.

"Then perhaps you already know what to say," he continued. "What you felt in the rickshaw, what you feel here at this table, this is the medicine. Not escaping the chaos, but finding calm inside it. Not running from life, but being fully in it."

Hansa felt her chest rise and fall more easily. For the first time in years, the thought of giving a talk did not make her nervous, it made her curious. She wanted to share this discovery, not as an expert, but as a fellow traveler.

She lifted her glass and drained the last sweet drop of chai, a quiet smile touching her lips. "Maybe," she said softly, "India really does transform you."

Kirit's eyes sparkled. "No, madam. India only shows you who you are."

Chapter Eight

Kirit caught the vendor's attention with a small wave of his hand. "Two more chais," he said with a grin, as though the first round had only been a warm-up. The vendor nodded, already pouring the amber liquid into two glasses that steamed in the afternoon air.

The sun had shifted higher, the heat pressing against the street with a weight that clung to skin and fabric alike, but the bustle around them never faltered. Cars nudged forward, horns played endlessly, motorbikes slipped through gaps no wider than a breath, and children darted past in bursts of laughter. Through it all, Kirit sat as if none of it touched him, his posture relaxed, his eyes carrying the same brightness that both unnerved and calmed Hansa at once.

When the chai arrived, he slid a glass toward her, the sides hot against her fingertips as she picked it up. They sat for a few quiet moments, sipping slowly, letting the sugared warmth coat their tongues. Then Kirit leaned forward slightly, his voice thoughtful.

"Tell me, madam," he said. "Do you remember everything that was behind the rickshaw while we drove?"

Hansa looked at him, startled by the question. She opened her mouth, then closed it, thinking. Her mind tried to pull the images together: the slum children, the goats wandering freely, the luxury cars, the cows in the middle of the road. She remembered flashes, fragments, but not all of it. And the truth was, she hadn't really thought of it at all until he asked.

"No," she admitted. "I don't. I remember some things, but once they were gone… they were gone. I was only watching what was in front of me."

Kirit nodded, as though this was exactly the answer he expected. He rested his elbows on the table, his hands curling around his chai glass. "Yes. That is the way it should be. But do you see how different it is for most of us in life? We keep looking behind us. We keep carrying what has already passed. Every turn, every stumble, every wrong road, we gather them up and place them on our shoulders. We drag the past with us as if it still belongs to us. And so, we live not in the road ahead, not in the now, but in the ghosts of what was."

Hansa tilted her head, the words settling into her. "Ghosts," she repeated softly.

Kirit's eyes glimmered. "Yes, madam. Ghosts. Tell me, when you sit alone at night, do you think only of the day that has just finished? Or do you think of years ago, failures, arguments, the ones you loved who left, the mistakes you believe you made?"

His words pierced straight through her. She shifted in her seat. Images flooded unbidden into her mind: her ex-husband's harsh words the night he left; the endless nights of sitting by her mother's bedside as dementia stole her piece by piece; the strained phone calls with her children who always sounded distracted, always needing to hang up. Even the small things came back, old slights, forgotten arguments, regrets about what she had said, what she hadn't.

"Yes," she whispered. "I think about them all the time. I can't seem to stop."

Kirit nodded gently, not in judgment but in understanding. "This is the curse of human beings. Animals do not live this way. A dog may be beaten, but the next day it will still wag its tail if kindness is shown. A bird will not sit on a branch thinking of the storm that broke its nest last season. They learn, they adjust, they continue. Only we humans sit with our ghosts, feeding them, calling them back into the present again and again. We carry the dead weight of things that no longer exist."

Hansa swallowed hard. She had never thought of it like that before. "But isn't it important to remember? To learn from what's happened?"

"Of course," Kirit replied. "But to learn is not the same as to cling. To see a mistake, to take its lesson, and then release it—that is wisdom. But what do we do? We take the mistake, we hold it close, and we whisper to it every night. We say, *you are mine, you define me, you are who I am.* That is not learning, madam. That is imprisonment."

The words fell heavy between them.

Kirit continued, his voice low and steady, as if weaving a spell. "The past is a road we have already traveled. Once the rickshaw has passed it, we cannot drive it again. We may look back for a moment to see where we came from, but if we stare too long, what happens?" He leaned forward, eyes locking with hers. "We crash. We lose sight of what is here, now, in front of us."

Hansa's breath caught. The metaphor was so simple, so obvious, and yet it struck her with a force she had not expected. She thought of her own life, how often she replayed conversations in her head, how many nights she had lain awake reliving her divorce, her mother's decline, her financial failures. Each memory was like a stone, and she had been carrying a mountain for years.

"Yes," she said quietly. "That's exactly what I do. I keep looking back. I keep… crashing."

Kirit smiled softly, not in triumph but in compassion. "It is not your fault. It is the way of many. We believe the past makes us who we are, and in some ways it does. But it is not meant to be carried forever. The past is meant to be a teacher, not a jailer."

He lifted his glass, taking another sip of chai before continuing. "Do you see how the ghosts work? They whisper when you are weakest. They tell you that you are still the person who failed, who lost, who suffered. But the truth, madam, is that those moments are gone. They cannot touch you now except through memory. You invite them in, and so they haunt you. But they are only shadows."

Hansa felt her eyes sting. She looked down at her hands, at the glass of chai warming her palms. How many years had she wasted living in the shadows of her past? How many mornings had she woken up already heavy with yesterday's grief?

She raised her gaze again, her voice trembling. "Then what am I supposed to do? How do I let go of the past?"

Kirit's answer was simple. "By being here. Now. Just as you were in the rickshaw."

He leaned closer, his words soft, almost like a chant. "Do you see? When you were watching the traffic, the colours, the people, you were only here. Not thinking of what had been. Not dragging your ghosts into the seat beside you. Just present. And in that present, you felt calm. Peaceful. Light. That is the truth, madam: peace does not come when life is quiet. Peace comes when you stop carrying what no longer exists."

The stall's vendor clattered dishes behind them, a boy ran past chasing a plastic ball, a beggar approached a nearby table and was handed a piece of bread without question. Life moved on in a constant tide, noisy and relentless. Yet in the centre of it all, Hansa felt as if something within her had gone utterly still.

Her mind, usually a whirlwind of thoughts, fell quiet as she considered his words. She thought of her mother's face in her final days, the sharp sting of her ex-husband's absence, the ache of children who seemed not to need her anymore. She realised these were not happening now. They belonged to roads already travelled. Yet she had brought them to this table, to this chai stall, carrying them like invisible luggage.

Tears appeared at the corners of her eyes, but they were not the tears of sorrow she was used to. They were lighter, almost cleansing. She set her glass down and pressed her hands together, not in prayer exactly, but in a gesture of gratitude, of surrender.

Kirit watched her silently, his expression unreadable, as though he had guided many travellers through this same lesson and knew that words could only take her so far. The rest was hers to discover.

Finally, she whispered, "So the rickshaw was the lesson."

Kirit smiled, his teeth flashing white against his tanned skin. "Yes, madam. The rickshaw was life. What is behind us is already gone. We cannot bring it back. We cannot drive it again. Only here, this moment, this breath, is real. And here, there is peace."

Hansa closed her eyes, letting the truth of it settle into her. For the first time in years, perhaps decades, she felt unshackled. The ghosts of her past still lingered, but they seemed smaller now, less powerful. All that mattered was the chai in her hands, the warmth of the cup, the hum of the street, and the steady presence of the man across from her.

When she opened her eyes again, her vision seemed sharper. The colours brighter. The world, alive and present, was waiting for her to join it—not as a prisoner of what was, but as herself, simply here.

And for the first time in a very long time, Hansa smiled.

Chapter Nine

The rickshaw's engine sputtered awake with a cough and a growl, the familiar vibrations traveling up through the worn leather seats as Kirit eased it back into the stream of traffic. Around them, Mumbai roared with its untamed music, horns bleating like stubborn goats, street vendors shouting above the noise, and the constant hum of engines jostling for space. Yet inside the rickshaw, Hansa felt cocooned, her body oddly at ease.

For a moment she simply watched the city swirl by, the saris blooming like flowers on the women who hurried past, the flash of gold bangles catching the sunlight, the bright painted signs with curling Devanagari script. Then Kirit spoke, his voice steady, almost casual, but carrying a weight she had begun to recognise.

"Madam," he said, eyes fixed on the road, "how are you feeling now, about your talk today?"

The question landed with surprising force. Last night, the thought of speaking before a hall of strangers had felt like a crushing stone on her chest. Her mind had spun in relentless circles: What if she forgot her words? What if the audience saw through her, saw the brokenness beneath the polished surface? What if they judged her for teaching about stress while she herself was unraveling? The anxiety had gnawed at her even as she lay in the hotel bed.

But now… she blinked, realising something that startled her. She hadn't thought about the talk all morning. Not while she'd dressed, not while she'd stepped into the chaos of the street, not during the chai with Kirit. Even now, she felt no tightness, no clenching fear.

She turned to him, almost amazed at her own words. "You know… I haven't really thought about it. Not once. Which is strange, because it has been worrying me since the moment I agreed to come."

Kirit's lips curved into that same serene smile, his eyes gleaming like sunlit water. "Ah," he said. "So the rickshaw has already been teaching you."

Hansa tilted her head, curious. "What do you mean?"

Kirit gestured lightly toward the chaos around them. "Look at this road. If, while driving, I only thought of the final destination, what would happen? My mind would race ahead, always imagining the place I must reach, worrying about when I will arrive. I would not see what is here. I would not notice the motorbike darting close, or the cow stepping out, or the boy running with his kite. My eyes would not be on this moment. And then…" He shrugged, lifting one hand from the handlebars briefly. "Accident."

Hansa nodded slowly. The simplicity of it was undeniable.

"But there is more," Kirit continued, weaving the rickshaw carefully between two honking taxis. "If I live only for the destination, I miss the beauty of the road itself. I would not stop for chai with you, I would not see the colours of the markets, I would not hear the music of the wedding procession passing by. All of this would be lost to me. Do you see? My mind would be trapped in an imaginary place, while life itself, real, beautiful, sacred, was passing me by."

His words sank deep into her chest, stirring something that had long lain dormant. She stared at the blur of colours rushing past: marigolds piled high on a cart, a splash of vermilion powder on a shrine, the vivid blue of a wall hand-painted with gods and advertisements. India was alive, vibrant in a way that demanded presence.

Kirit's voice lowered, more serious now. "This is the way of anxiety, madam. We imagine, we assume. We create entire worlds in our minds, full of disasters that have not yet come. We say, *what if I fail, what if they reject me, what if I am not enough?* We believe these thoughts are real, and so our bodies suffer as if they are real. Heart races, stomach tightens, sleep disappears. But look around you now." He gestured at the crowded street. "Where is this fear? Can you touch it? Can you see it? No. It is only a shadow made by the mind."

Hansa felt a shiver run through her. He was right. The stress she had carried for weeks about this talk had existed nowhere except in her own head. Yet it had stolen her peace, her health, her joy. She had been living in a false world, one conjured from assumptions.

Kirit glanced at her. "Do you know, madam, how many people ruin their lives because of assumptions? They imagine their husband will leave them, so they grow bitter before he ever does. They assume a business will fail, so they never even begin. They think others are judging them, so they hide their true selves. And all the while, nothing has actually happened. They suffer from ghosts of the future, just as from ghosts of the past."

Hansa thought of her own life. The nights spent replaying conversations, imagining what her colleagues thought of her, worrying that her children blamed her for everything, picturing herself failing before she even began. How many opportunities had she walked away from because she assumed the outcome would be failure? How many friendships had withered because she assumed she wasn't wanted?

She felt a lump rise in her throat. "Yes," she murmured. "I've done that. More times than I can count. I've destroyed things before they even had a chance to live."

Kirit's tone softened. "We all do. But in India, you see another way. Here, life is so full, so loud, so immediate, that it demands you stay present. Look around you: the man in the slum and the man in the Mercedes, both eating samosas side by side. The woman carrying water on her head while talking on a mobile phone. The cow lying in the middle of the road, while traffic parts around it as if it were a king. This is India. It teaches you that life cannot be controlled or predicted. It can only be lived."

The rickshaw jolted over a pothole, but Kirit remained steady, his hands sure on the handlebars. He seemed to move with the flow rather than against it, his body relaxed, his eyes bright. Hansa watched him, marvelling. How could he remain so calm in this chaos? And yet, wasn't this chaos a mirror of her own life?

Noise, disorder, unpredictability, and still, somehow, there was a rhythm, a beauty, if one surrendered to it.

Kirit spoke again, his words like a mantra woven into the hum of the city. "The misery of assumption, madam, is that it blinds us to reality. We are so busy fearing the storm we imagine, we do not see the clear sky above us. We miss the laughter of a child, the kindness of a stranger, the beauty of a marigold garland. We walk through paradise, yet believe we are in hell."

Hansa felt her chest loosen. Tears welled in her eyes, not of sorrow, but of recognition, of awakening. She had spent so much of her life lost in imagined worlds of despair. Even last night, she had been paralysed with fear about today. And yet here she was, breathing, alive, being carried through a city of impossible vitality. The fear had not come true. It had never even existed outside her mind.

She whispered, almost to herself, "So all those nights I lay awake… all that suffering… it was only me, wasn't it? I did it to myself."

Kirit gave a small nod. "Yes. But do not blame yourself. This is what humans do. The mind is a storyteller, always inventing, always warning, always trying to protect. But we forget that these stories are not real. And so we live in them, missing the reality that is right in front of us."

The rickshaw wove around a bullock cart piled with sugarcane, past a man singing bhajans with a small drum, past women selling strings of jasmine flowers on the roadside. Life spilled over every corner, messy and sacred all at once.

"India heals," Kirit said softly. "Not because it removes the chaos, but because it shows you how to live within it. Here, contradictions live side by side, poverty and wealth, noise and silence, suffering and joy. You cannot control it. You can only be present with it. And in that presence, there is peace."

Hansa closed her eyes for a moment, letting the sounds and smells wash over her: the spice of frying pakoras, the sweetness of incense wafting from a temple, the sharp honk of a truck horn painted with *Horn OK*

Please. She let it all be as it was, not pushing it away, not wishing it different. For the first time, she understood what it meant to simply exist, to simply be.

When she opened her eyes, the world seemed brighter, sharper, more alive. She turned to Kirit, her voice steady but full of wonder. "All morning, I have not thought about my talk. And now that I do, I find I am not afraid. It will come as it comes. I don't need to live it before it happens."

Kirit's smile widened, his face glowing with quiet joy. "Yes, madam. You are in the rickshaw now. You are here."

And as the little vehicle rattled through the vibrant, chaotic streets of Mumbai, Hansa felt something inside her loosen and fall away—an old weight she had carried far too long. She leaned back against the seat, her body soft, her heart strangely light. The talk no longer mattered in the way it once had. What mattered was this: the chai still warm in her stomach, the city alive around her, and the presence of a man who drove a rickshaw as though it were a temple on wheels.

For the first time in years, perhaps decades, she was not living in the past, nor in the shadows of what might be. She was here. Alive. Present.

And it was enough.

Chapter Ten

The traffic thickened as they drew closer to the venue. Rickshaws pressed in from every angle, taxis honked impatiently, motorbikes darted like dragonflies between lorries painted in garish shades of blue and green. Yet despite the chaos, there was no sense of fury in the air. The horns were not sharp stabs of anger but rather part of the music of movement, like signals in a dance where everyone somehow knew their steps.

Hansa leaned slightly forward, gripping the edge of the rickshaw as another car nosed boldly into their path. She expected Kirit to curse, to slam his fist on the handlebar, to mutter angrily under his breath. But he didn't. Instead, he simply slowed a little, let the car ease in, and then adjusted his course without a ripple of frustration. His face remained calm, almost serene; as if he had known all along that this was how it would unfold.

She shook her head, marvelling. "How is it," she asked, "that everyone just keeps moving? Nobody seems to get angry, even when people cut across or push their way in. Where I live, this would have caused road rage. People would be shouting, swearing, maybe worse. But here… it's like nobody takes offence."

Kirit's eyes sparkled as he glanced at her. "Because, madam, this is India. Here, we know that obstacles, interruptions, delays. They are all part of the road. Why should we become angry at what is natural? A goat may wander into the street, a child may chase his ball, a car may cut across. If I fight every obstruction, if I waste my energy shouting at each one, then the road becomes unbearable. But if I accept them as part of the journey, then it is only movement. Only life."

He paused, weaving neatly around a bicycle piled high with metal pots that clanged like temple bells. Then he continued.

"Life is the same. Every day brings hurdles, financial troubles, quarrels in family, sickness in the body, disappointments in work. Sometimes they creep slowly, like a relationship that drains you little by little, and sometimes they cut sharply, like being suddenly dismissed from your job. But however they come, they are part of the road. If I stop and fight each one, I waste my strength. I stop moving. I give my energy to what is not worth it."

Hansa listened, transfixed. The analogy struck home with painful clarity. How many times had she wasted her energy pushing back against what life threw at her, cursing her misfortunes, replaying them in her mind, resisting what had already come?

Kirit continued, his voice like the low chant of a prayer woven into the roar of traffic. "You see, madam, if I tried to argue with every driver, if I shouted each time someone cut me off, I would arrive nowhere. My energy would be burned up in anger. Instead, I go with the current. I give way when I must, and others give way to me in time. Look, " He gestured ahead, where another rickshaw slid in front of them. "I allow him through. It is not a race. I will arrive when I arrive, and that moment will be the perfect moment for me. And when it is my turn to move forward, others will part like the sea, letting me pass without anger, without debt. This is the dance of the road. And this, too, is the dance of life."

The words moved through Hansa like a gentle current. She thought of her years struggling alone, of how fiercely she had fought against every difficulty, her husband leaving, the loneliness of raising children without gratitude, the crushing bills, the long decline of her mother. Each time, she had clenched her fists, battled the pain, resisted what already was. And where had it brought her? Only exhaustion, only a life lived in constant strain.

Kirit manoeuvred the rickshaw around a pothole wide as a pond. "When you fight the river, madam, you drown. When you let the river carry you, you float. That is the wisdom of India. Here, we say everything is written, *kismat*, destiny. This does not mean we are helpless. It means the path is already there beneath our feet. You may walk it in anger, with a heavy heart, or you may walk it in acceptance, with joy. The path will not change, but your experience of it can be bliss or misery. That choice is yours."

Hansa felt her chest tighten and release. Bliss or misery. Hadn't she chosen misery without realising it? By resisting, by clinging, by fighting every twist of the road?

Kirit gestured at the flow of traffic around them. "See this, madam. This chaos is like life itself. There are distractions everywhere, horns, animals, people crossing, vendors shouting. If I worry about why a man shouts, or where a cow comes from, or whether this bus will move faster or slower, then I am lost. I cannot see what is here, now. Better to keep my eyes open, remain calm, and let life flow. Distractions are part of the journey. But if I do not feed them with my attention, they pass like clouds."

They passed a small temple wedged between two high buildings. The scent of burning incense drifted into the rickshaw, mingling with exhaust and spice. A man in a white dhoti bowed before the deity, touching his forehead to the ground while buses thundered by just feet away. The contrast struck Hansa deeply. This quiet act of devotion in the middle of the chaos.

Kirit must have sensed her gaze. "This is India," he said softly. "Spirituality is not separate from daily life here. It is not found only in temples or ashrams, but in the streets, in the food stalls, in the traffic. It is the way a driver gives way without anger, the way a beggar shares half his bread with a stray dog, the way rich and poor sit side by side drinking the same chai. All of it teaches the same lesson: surrender. Flow. Acceptance. To live without clinging, without fighting, without fear."

Hansa felt her throat ache, her eyes filling with tears. She remembered how she had sat last night in the hotel, her heart pounding, her mind filled with dread about her talk. She had imagined humiliation, failure, rejection. She had fought against the very idea of it. And yet here she was now, carried by this city, this rickshaw, this man who seemed to embody serenity itself and the fear had vanished like mist under the morning sun.

"Do you see?" Kirit said gently. "It is not the obstacles that cause our suffering. It is our resistance. The road will always have bumps, animals, drivers who cut across. But if I keep moving, if I allow what comes and then let it pass, there is no suffering. Only movement. Only flow. Only life."

The rickshaw swerved gently, avoiding a woman balancing a bundle of firewood on her head. Hansa watched her disappear into the crowd, her sari glowing bright against the gray dust of the street. The words echoed in her mind: *Only movement. Only life.*

She turned to Kirit, her voice hushed. "And you believe all of this is written? That even the obstacles are meant to be?"

"Yes," he said simply. "We believe that destiny is already woven. You cannot escape it, any more than I can escape the shape of this road. But what I can choose is how I drive it. With anger, or with peace. With fear, or with trust. That is where freedom lies. That is where joy lives. Indians say, *sab kuch likha hai*—everything is written. So why not smile as you read the page?"

Hansa let the words settle into her heart. She thought of her years of resistance, of anger, of sorrow. All along, the road had been set before her. Perhaps the only mistake had been in how she had walked it, with clenched fists and eyes fixed on what she had lost, rather than what she still had.

As the Bombay Exhibition Centre came into view, gleaming white against the sprawl of the city, Hansa felt no fear. No dread. Only a quiet recognition that she would arrive when she was meant to arrive, and that moment would be the perfect moment. The talk would be what it would be. The audience would receive it as they were meant to receive it. All she had to do was keep moving, keep flowing, keep being present.

The rickshaw rattled to a halt at the gates, the noise of the crowd swelling around them. Hansa placed her hand briefly over Kirit's on the handlebars, her eyes wet with gratitude. "Thank you," she whispered.

Kirit bowed his head slightly, his smile serene. "No need, madam. It is only the road teaching its lessons. I am only the driver."

And as Hansa stepped out into the bustle of the conference, she carried with her not fear, not anxiety, but the quiet wisdom of the rickshaw: life was not a race, not a battle. It was a current, a wave, a river to be ridden with a calm heart and a smile on her face.

Chapter Eleven

Hansa stepped down from the rickshaw, her hand lingering on the cool metal frame for just a moment. She turned to Kirit, her chest swelling with gratitude. "Thank you," she said softly, her voice almost lost in the noise of the crowd surging around the gates of the Bombay Exhibition Centre.

Kirit gave her that warm, serene smile that had become so familiar in only a few hours together. It was a smile that seemed to hold no strain, no rush, no heaviness, only the simple acceptance of life as it unfolded. Hansa felt it radiate into her, calming her heart as surely as the steady hum of a chant.

Then, suddenly, like a blow from nowhere, panic seized her chest. Her breath caught in her throat. Her hands grew clammy.

"My notes!" she gasped. Her bag felt lighter, too light. She fumbled inside, rifling through the contents with shaking fingers. Lipstick. Wallet. Passport. But no folder, no carefully written pages she had spent nights scribbling, crafting, rehearsing. Her heart began to pound so violently she thought it might burst through her ribs.

"They're still at the hotel," she whispered, horror rising like a tide. "I left them on the desk. All my notes, everything I planned to say."

The edges of her vision seemed to blur. Sweat prickled at her hairline. She could almost see herself standing in front of hundreds of strangers, tonguetied, blank, exposed. The fear she had thought she had conquered surged back with merciless force.

She looked at Kirit, her voice breaking. "What am I going to do? I can't... I can't do this without my notes."

He didn't rush to answer. Instead, he placed his hand gently on her shoulder. It was a simple gesture, yet the moment his palm rested there, Hansa felt something extraordinary. A warmth spreading from the point of contact, flowing through her body like sunlight breaking into a cold, dark room.

The panic didn't vanish instantly, but it softened, dulled, as though she were being pulled back from the edge of a cliff. Her breath steadied, her vision cleared. She looked at Kirit's calm face and felt a stillness settle inside her, as if she had tapped into a wellspring of peace that had always been there, waiting.

His smile widened just slightly, his eyes kind. "Madam," he said, "this is no different than the traffic."

Hansa blinked, trying to grasp his meaning.

"When another driver cuts across, should I stop my rickshaw in anger? Should I shout, fight, waste my energy? No. I keep going. I adjust, I flow, I trust the road. And soon enough, I find my way again. This moment, your forgotten notes, is only like that. A sudden cut across your path. You must not stop. You must not fight. Keep moving, and the road will carry you where you must go."

His words washed over her, steadying her pulse. She breathed deeply, the air thick with exhaust and incense from a nearby temple, and nodded.

Then Kirit did something that startled her. He slipped a bracelet from his wrist and held it out to her.

It was made of small, round, brown beads, each textured with intricate ridges, strung together with a simple red thread.

"This," he said, placing it gently in her palm, "is a rudraksha."

Hansa turned it over in her hands, fascinated. The beads were light yet somehow solid, carrying an energy she could feel pulsing faintly against her skin.

Kirit's voice grew reverent. "Rudraksha comes from the sacred tree, its seeds worn for thousands of years by sages and seekers. They say Lord Shiva himself wept tears that became the rudraksha, filled with divine energy. It calms the mind, protects the heart, and anchors the spirit into the present. This one has been with me many years, through many roads. Now it is yours."

Hansa looked up, startled. "I can't take this from you. It's yours."

Kirit shook his head slowly. "No, madam. Today it is yours. Wear it when you speak. Hold it in your hand, and it will remind you that everything you need is already here"—he touched her chest, just over her heart—"rooted deep inside. The universe does not abandon those who stay present. It flows through them, gives them strength, gives them words. But if your mind runs away into the past, or chases fears of the future, then you lose that current. You stand alone, cut off. Stay here. Stay now. And the universe will speak through you."

Hansa's throat ached with emotion. She slid the bracelet over her wrist. It felt surprisingly natural there, as though it had been waiting for her all along. The beads were warm against her skin, grounding her, reminding her of chai stalls, roadside samosas, the laughter of slum children, the calm of riding through chaos with this remarkable man.

She breathed deeply. The panic ebbed further, replaced by a trembling, fragile confidence.

As she adjusted the strap of her bag, she turned back to him. "Can you... can you pick me up again at midday? For the return journey?"

"Of course," Kirit said simply. "I will be here."

He revved the rickshaw's engine and began to pull away. As the vehicle disappeared into the current of traffic, Hansa's eyes caught on something painted in curling letters across the back.

KHIARNISTA.

She frowned. What did it mean? A name? A word? A secret? She smiled faintly to herself. She would ask him later.

Turning back to the looming façade of the Bombay Exhibition Centre, her heart pounded, not with panic this time, but with anticipation. She touched the rudraksha bracelet lightly, as though drawing courage from it, and stepped through the gates.

The lights were blinding.

Hansa stood at the podium, her body stiff, her throat dry. Hundreds of eyes were on her, the auditorium filled with a sea of faces, some curious, some skeptical, all waiting. The hum of the air-conditioning blended with the faint, sweet scent of incense that still clung to her senses. She gripped the edges of the podium, her knuckles white.

For a moment, fear threatened again. The old familiar voice rose in her head: *You don't have your notes. You'll forget everything. They'll see you're a fraud. You're not ready.*

Her breath faltered.

But then her fingers brushed against the rudraksha bracelet. She closed her hand around it, feeling the ridged beads press into her skin, grounding her. She remembered Kirit's hand on her shoulder, the warmth that had poured through her, the calm in his eyes. She remembered his words: *Stay here. Stay now.*

She inhaled deeply. The scent of incense filled her lungs. The chatter in her mind quieted. A smile spread slowly across her lips.

And then, without hesitation, she spoke.

"To combat stress," she said, her voice steady, clear, surprising even herself, "ride a rickshaw."

A ripple of laughter moved through the audience, warm, inviting. Hansa felt the tension in her shoulders release. The words that followed did not come from notes, nor from rehearsed lines, but from something deeper, something rooted within her.

"To combat stress," Hansa repeated, letting the playful rhythm of the words settle in the room, "ride a rickshaw."

The audience chuckled again, their attention sharpened. Hansa smiled back, her nerves dissolving with each heartbeat. "Yes, I mean it. It sounds strange, doesn't it?

But this morning I learned more about stress—and how to release it—while sitting in the back of a rattling little rickshaw on the streets of Mumbai than I ever learned in years of study or even in leading workshops."

She paused, allowing the silence to expand, to breathe. She could see people leaning forward now, curious.

"In my life, stress has been my constant companion. Divorce, raising two children alone, caring for my mother until her last breath, watching my finances crumble, my health weaken, my smile disappear... stress has been the background noise to everything. It has been like a shadow, always chasing me, always whispering: *you are not enough, you are failing, you are late, you are weak."*

Her throat caught, but she gripped the rudraksha bracelet and continued.

"And yet... in that rickshaw, surrounded by chaos like I had never seen before—horns blaring, cars cutting across, people walking in front of vehicles, animals wandering, vendors selling, children playing in the streets—I felt something extraordinary. I felt calm."

She let that sink in.

"I realised then that stress is not in the noise. Stress is not in the chaos. Stress is not in the bills, the deadlines, the demands of family or work. Stress is in how we *hold* it all, in how we resist, in how we live everywhere but here, in this moment. Stress is born when we drag behind us the heavy chains of the past, or when we race ahead into an imagined future filled with problems that may never come. Stress is the ghost-world we build in our own minds, while life itself—this incredible, unpredictable life—is happening right here, right now."

A murmur moved through the audience. Heads nodded.

She gestured lightly with her hands, growing more animated, more alive. "As the rickshaw weaved through traffic, I realized I didn't remember every car, every obstacle that had been behind us. The moment they were gone, they were gone. That is the past. Yet how many of us keep looking back, holding on, carrying our failures, our regrets, our heartbreaks? We live them again and again, though they are already gone.

And when I worried about this talk last night, I was living in a world that didn't even exist. I imagined myself failing. I imagined forgetting my words. I imagined disappointment, judgment, shame. But none of that was real. They were only shadows in my mind, feeding fear.

The truth is, life only exists here—in this breath, this heartbeat, this step, this smile. And when we live here, we find peace. Even in the middle of the loudest chaos."

She could see the effect her words were having. Some listeners closed their eyes. Others exchanged glances, visibly moved. She pressed on, her voice stronger now.

"I asked the rickshaw driver, Kirit, how he managed to stay so calm while driving in such madness. Do you know what he said? He told me that if he kept his eyes fixed only on the final destination, he would lose the present moment. He would miss what was happening now. And then he would crash."

She allowed the analogy to land.

"Isn't that what we do in our lives? We fix our eyes on some faraway destination—a promotion, a perfect relationship, financial security, happiness—and we forget to notice what is happening right now. We miss the beauty of the road, the taste of the tea, the smile of a stranger, the blessing of one calm breath. And worse, we stumble. We crash into life because our minds are not here with us."

Her tone softened. "This morning, Kirit stopped his rickshaw at a roadside stall because, he said, he heard my stomach rumbling." A ripple of laughter. Hansa smiled. "Yes, he did. Somehow, in the middle of all that noise, he heard. And he fed me samosas and chai. And there I saw something that would be unthinkable in many places: a man stepping out of a luxury car sat at the same plastic table as a man from the slums. Both enjoying the same food, the same laughter, the same life.

That is India. That is why people say this country transforms you. Because it shows you that separation is an illusion. Rich or poor, strong or weak, we all share this present moment. Side by side, the waves of life carry us together."

She touched the rudraksha on her wrist, drawing strength from its rough beads.

"Stress makes us believe we are alone in our suffering. But the truth is, we are never alone. The universe flows through us and around us. When we surrender to it, when we stop resisting, when we stop clutching to the past or fearing the future, life holds us. Just as the traffic here in Mumbai—messy as it looks—somehow flows, we too are carried when we let go.

The harder we fight, the more energy we waste. The more we surrender, the more we see that life itself is guiding us."

Her voice dropped into a near-whisper. "So I say again: to combat stress, ride a rickshaw. Let it teach you that chaos can be beautiful, that calm can exist in the middle of noise, that peace is not in controlling life, but in flowing with it. Let it show you that every breath is enough, every step is enough, and that you, right here, right now, are enough."

And as the audience leaned in, listening, some smiling, some nodding, Hansa realised that the words were not hers alone. They rose like a tide through her, carried by something larger, something infinite. The universe was speaking, just as Kirit had promised, flowing through her as effortlessly as the rickshaw through Mumbai's streets.

The room was silent now, reverent, as though the audience was collectively holding its breath. Hansa let her words rest there, unhurried, like a leaf floating down to still water.

Then she smiled, a true, unforced smile, the kind she thought she had lost forever. "Thank you."

The hall erupted in applause, the sound rising like a wave. Hansa bowed her head slightly, overwhelmed, the bracelet warm on her wrist, the scent of incense still in her lungs.

And for the first time in many, many years, she felt light.
She felt alive.

She felt free.

Final Chapter

Hansa walked out of the Bombay Exhibition Centre as though her feet were no longer tethered to the earth. The air outside was thick with heat, traffic fumes, and the ever-present orchestra of horns, yet none of it weighed on her. She felt lighter than she had in decades, as though the heavy stones she had been carrying in her chest, stones of regret, loneliness, fear, exhaustion, had at last been set down.

She breathed deeply, and for the first time in years, her lungs felt like wings.

It was not just that the talk had gone well. It was something far deeper. This time, she had not spoken from borrowed knowledge, not from the rehearsed notes of books or courses she had once leaned upon like a crutch. She had spoken from her own lived experience. From the trembling truth of her own heart.

And the audience had heard it. She could still see their faces in her mind's eye, eyes wide, lips parted, heads nodding, people leaning forward as if her words were not merely passing sounds but sparks of recognition. She had not taught them from above; she had walked beside them, hand in hand, sharing her own struggles and the strange, beautiful lessons of the morning.

She smiled to herself. *It was the rickshaw*, she thought. *It was always the rickshaw.*

The image made her laugh softly, joy bubbling up in her chest. She wanted to tell someone, to share her gratitude, her wonder, her amazement at the way life had unfolded. And she knew exactly who she wanted to tell—her children.

The thought of them no longer carried the sting of resentment it once did. For years she had nursed a quiet wound, aching for appreciation, frustrated that they only called when she did, blind to all she had sacrificed. But today, as she replayed the lessons Kirit had given her, she saw things differently.

Traffic, she thought. *That's all it is. The way they cut across, or hold back, or ignore me—it's just traffic. I don't need to fight it, I don't need to take it personally. I can simply give way, let them pass, and keep moving.*

Her heart swelled. As soon as she got back to the hotel, she would call them, not to ask for thanks, not to plead for recognition, but simply to tell them she loved them. And whether they responded warmly or not at all, it wouldn't matter. She wasn't clinging anymore. She was giving way to traffic.

The thought made her feel as though she were floating on air.

Her eyes scanned the street outside the conference centre. And then she saw it, parked exactly where she had been dropped off that morning, the rickshaw. Her rickshaw. The sight of it filled her with excitement, almost childlike in its intensity. She wanted to run to it, to tell Kirit everything: how the talk had gone, how the audience had laughed and nodded, how she had spoken freely, fearlessly, because of him.

She wanted to tell him he had been the star of her talk, that it was his wisdom, his calm, his presence that had carried her through.

She quickened her pace, smiling, her bag bouncing against her side. But as she drew closer, her steps faltered. Something was wrong.

The man in the driver's seat was not Kirit.

She blinked, confused. Perhaps Kirit had stepped away, she thought. Maybe this was another driver minding the vehicle for him. But the man was clearly waiting for her, hands resting lightly on the handlebars, eyes scanning the crowd as though searching for his passenger.

When he saw her approach, he smiled politely. "Madam?" he asked. "Your hotel?"

Hansa hesitated. "Yes… but where is the other driver?"

The driver looked puzzled. "Other driver?"

"Yes," Hansa said, her voice urgent now. "The man who drove me here this morning. Where is he?"

The driver frowned, genuinely confused. "Madam, I do not know what you mean. I was the one who picked you up this morning. From your hotel. I dropped you here for your conference. And now I am here to take you back. As you asked."

Hansa's brow furrowed. "No. No, you didn't. I remember him clearly. We stopped for samosas and chai at a roadside stall. We talked about stress, about life."

The driver shook his head firmly. "No, madam. That cannot be. It is against our company policy to stop for food with passengers. We pick up, we drop off. Nothing else. I assure you, I was the one who brought you here."

A ripple of unease spread through Hansa. Her mouth grew dry. She turned, almost desperately, and looked at the back of the rickshaw. The same painted letters stared back at her: *KHIARNISTA*.

It was the same rickshaw. She hadn't imagined that.

Her pulse quickened. She returned to the driver, her voice trembling. "Listen. This morning, I rode in this very rickshaw. But the driver was Kirit. We spoke. We laughed. He gave me this" she held up her wrist, showing him the rudraksha bracelet. "His name was Kirit!"

The driver's eyes widened slightly, unease flickering across his face. He swallowed. "Kirit?" he repeated slowly.

"Yes," Hansa said, relief flooding her that at least he recognised the name. "Kirit. Do you know him?"

The driver shifted uncomfortably, glancing at the ground. Then, with a heavy sigh, he nodded. "Yes, madam. I know the name. But... you must understand something. This rickshaw, the one you sit in now, it was built and driven by my great-grandfather. His name was Kirit."

Hansa stared, stunned into silence.

"My great-grandfather was known in these streets," the driver continued, his voice low, almost reverent. "He was calm, always smiling, never in a rush, never angry.

People said he had the patience of a saint. He taught many lessons to those who rode with him. But, madam…" He hesitated, his eyes lifting to meet hers. "He died many, many years ago."

The world seemed to tilt. Hansa's breath caught in her chest. She shook her head, unable to process the words. "No," she whispered. "No, that's not possible. I met him. I spoke to him. I touched him. He gave me this bracelet."

The driver's gaze softened with a mixture of curiosity and awe. "Madam, my great-grandfather's name was Kirit. And yes, he wore a rudraksha bracelet always. People said it kept him connected to the divine."

He reached across the dashboard and pointed. Hansa followed his gesture. There, tucked into the corner of the driver's side, was a small black-and-white photograph, faded with age.

Her breath stopped.

It was Kirit.

The same serene smile. The same folded hands. The same bright, calm eyes that had disarmed her fear and filled her with peace. And on his wrist—she saw it clearly, even in the old photo—the rudraksha bracelet.

Her hand flew to her mouth. Tears blurred her vision.

The driver looked at her with quiet wonder. "I do not know what you experienced, madam. But many people say he was more than just a man. They say his spirit lived on in his rickshaw, guiding those who needed him, comforting those in pain. Perhaps..." He hesitated, his voice dropping. "Perhaps he came to you because you were ready. Because you needed him."

Hansa could not speak. Her chest ached with emotion, with awe, with gratitude. She touched the bracelet on her wrist, the beads pressing firmly into her skin.

She thought of his words: *Stay here. Stay now. The universe will help you.*

Her tears fell freely, but they were not heavy tears. They were light, cleansing, like the first rain after a long drought.

She looked once more at the photograph, at the man who had guided her through chaos, who had taught her to surrender, to flow, to live. And she whispered softly, "Thank you, Kirit."

The driver did not hear her, but perhaps the universe did.

She stepped into the rickshaw, the same seat where she had sat that morning, and as it pulled away from the Exhibition Centre, she closed her eyes. The horns blared, the traffic surged, the city swirled with noise and colour, but inside her, there was only stillness.

For the first time in her life, Hansa was truly free.

In conclusion

Kirit Thakore has been transforming lives physically for over 30 years, as he has been a fitness instructor most of his life. Martial arts, boxing, body transformation and HIIT training have all played a big part. His big break came in 2015, when he developed a fitness workout based on Bhangra (Punjabi folk dance). This skyrocketed him and earned him a TV series based on fitness, a major headlining performance at the Manchester Indoor Arena on the eve of the India vs Pakistan world cup cricket match as well as having 100's of instructors all over the UK delivering his workouts.

This came to a standstill overnight as the world stopped due to COVID.

Kirit had not only been transforming peoples bodies, he had also been transforming their lives with positivity and helping them create an "I can" attitude.

He has always been a deeply spiritual person and visited ashrams around the world to get more of an understanding, but realised the only way to truly know, was to experience.

Kirit's first book was born from tragedy as it was based on his personal lived experience of his beloved mother struggling with dementia. When she passed away in 1990, his world was shattered and the only way he could grieve was to write down all his feelings. Good experiences and bad. To truly realise them. This resulted in his incredibly powerful and very emotional book "If I only knew then, what I know now about DEMENTIA". This book is a something everyone should read. It will help those who have struggled with it heal and it will others recognise symptoms.

His next book was again based on his lived experience. This time on the impact that testosterone deficiency has on a man. At 50, Kirit's life changed. He was eating healthy, exercising and had no worries, yet over a very short period of time, everything inside of him was going wrong. This book shares intimate details of Kirit's battle with himself and with the medical system. All men should read this as it will effect the majority. The ones who are being affected now, will find a solution that will make them feel alive again.

He then went on to write 2 further books. One on weight loss and the other about daily spiritual habits that Kirit practices himself.

The Happy Rickshaw Driver is something he enjoyed so much writing about as it is the perfect example of how he lives his life. He states that when he read it himself, he felt a sense of calm, total joy and the odd tear, as it is a reflection of much of his life.

You will never see Kirit without a Rudraksha bracelet on. Everyone has spiritual and deep meaning for these, but for him, they are there to ground him, just like Hansa when she was on stage. Any time he feels any kind of pressure, he places his hand on his wrist, closes his eyes, takes a breath and he is back in that rickshaw.

If you would like one of these bracelets, Kirit brought a number from a temple in India. They are not expensive, as not bought for profit. If you would like one, please email him directly at kirit.thakore@gmail.com.

Did you work out what KHIARNISTA is?

For more information on Kirit and his life, please goto kirit.uk

From the Author

Thank you for taking a moment of your life reading this book and about me. For a moment you were in the present with me and that means so much. At the completion of this book my 4th grandchild and 1st grand daughter was born. My words are my legacy to my children, grand children and as Kirit, The Happy Rickshaw Driver, is, I'm hoping a legacy to great great grand children too.

"The effect you have on others is the most valuable currency there is." Jim Carrey

Kirit Thakore

www.ingramcontent.com/pod-product-compliance
Lightning Source LLC
Chambersburg PA
CBHW011421070526
44584CB00026BA/3786